I0474459

The A-Z of Digital Marketing

(buzzwords and jargon to help turn you into a digital unicorn)

by

James Gaubert

PublishNation
www.publishnation.co.uk

Introduction

It doesn't matter if you are just starting a career in digital marketing or, if like me, you are a seasoned veteran. The world we live in today is digitally driven and developing at a pace never seen before.

New innovations, acronyms, platforms, tools and methodology are appearing almost on a daily basis, with this in mind I decided to create a single source of information to help explain some of the common terminology and to help people better understand some of the fundamentals.

It goes without saying that by the time I have had this book published I will probably need to start writing a second edition, but in the meantime I hope this goes a little way to helping you understand some of the jargon that is used today!

What qualifies me to write this book I hear you ask. 2018 marks my 20th anniversary working in the field of digital marketing, and believe me I have seen a lot of changes over the past 20 years.

I have worked across numerous markets including London and Europe, Dubai and the Middle East and more recently Malaysia and APAC. These markets have all been at different maturity levels when it comes to digital marketing and whilst I have had the privilege of working with some incredible people I have often had to explain and educate as I go!

I would consider myself to be a solid digital generalist. What I mean by this is that I have had the fortune of working across multiple disciplines. I have run multiple digital marketing agencies, including those that are part of large global groups and also small independent boutiques. In these roles I have been lucky enough to work with some of the world's leading brands on projects based around social media, website design and build, eCommerce, Mobile, Search and SEO, Media, Data, Analytics, even innovative tech like Artificial Intelligence, Augmented Reality and 3D printing.

But enough about me! Let's get cracking with my current, and at time of print, complete A-Z of digital marketing, everything you need to know to become a digital unicorn!

One, Two, Three...

3D Printing

3D Printing is the process of making three dimensional solid objects from a digital file. The creation of a 3D printed object is achieved using additive processes. In an additive process an object is created by laying down successive layers of material until the object is created. Each of these layers can be seen as a thinly sliced horizontal cross-section of the eventual object. 3D printing is the opposite of subtractive manufacturing which is cutting out / hollowing out a piece of metal or plastic with for instance a milling machine. 3D printing enables you to produce complex shapes using less material than traditional manufacturing methods.

360 Campaigns

A 360 campaign covers the entire buying cycle/path to purchase, from discovery through to repeat purchase. Every medium is used although today there is a heavy reliance on digital and social. Ensuring that as a brand you provide a consistent experience throughout your 360 campaign is key, synergy from branding through to messaging across platforms and technology to help drive the consumer down the path to purchase. Data also plays a very important role in 360 campaigns, using data smartly will help ensure that you are sending the right message to the right people on the right device at the right time!

A is for Apple

A/B Testing

A/B testing, or sometimes called split testing, isn't actually anything new. However, thanks to the transparency and ability to analyze activity using digital channels this practice has become the norm! A/B testing is best described as the act of running a simultaneous comparison/experiment between two different platforms. For example if you are building a landing page you may want to split test two different page layouts, in fact you don't have to limit the test to just two variants. A/B testing doesn't have to be limited to web pages either, you can split test emailers, ad copy, creative – pretty much anything you can think of!

Ad Blocker

An ad blocker is a piece of software/computer program that is used to remove different types of advertising from an internet users online experience. These programs typically target certain ad types, such as pop-ups, banner ads and other common forms of online/digital advertising. Why would we use an ad blocker? To ensure we have a quality online user experience without any intrusive distractions from ads!

Ad Builder

Ad Builder in an important element that sits within Google AdWords and is used to create ad content. The Ad builder tool is a logical continuation from selecting your keywords, allowing you to create ads specifically ad groups that you have setup. Ad builder doesn't just have to be used with text based PPC ads, in fact it really comes to life when sued to support image-based ads too. Google Display Network has hundreds of templates that can be used and gives you the opportunity to customize layouts, colors and fonts.

Ad Extensions

Ad extensions are essentially additional pieces of information about your brand or business, such as phone number, or even links to specific pages on your website, you can add to your PPC ads. There is no additional charge for setting up and using these extensions, with the usual charges for any clicks that you get through them. It is really important to include ad extensions as they can significantly improve the visibility of your ads, which can lead to more clicks and improve your overall ROI. The most popular extensions to include are call extensions, location extensions, app extensions, review extensions and price extensions.

Ad Server

In stark contrast to ad blocking, an ad server is software that stores data relating to online advertising content and then publishes and delivers the ads to websites, applications and ultimately to the end user. Ideal technology if you are looking to reach the masses!

AdSense

AdSense is an advertising platform from our friends over at Google. The AdSense program is specifically designed for website publishers who want to display targeted text, video or image advertisements on website pages and earn money when site visitors view or click on the ads. These ads are controlled and managed by Google and web publishers simply need to create a free AdSense account and copy and paste provided code to display the ads. Revenue using AdSense is generated on a per-click or per impression basis.

Advertainment

Advertainment is the mix between advertisement and entertainment, usually in an interactive engaging format. In many cases advertainment refers to particular media that combines forms of entertainment such as television, songs and movies, ultimately the goal is of course to promote a brand!

Advocacy

Advocacy in digital marketing terms is best described as the approach to engaging your audience online and inspiring them to take action around your brand. One of the best platforms to build advocacy is social media, in many cases followers of your brand on social are already advocates, the trick is how to use them to help amplify your message.

AdWords

This is the first of several Google related elements in this A-Z, and one of my personal favorites. AdWords is essentially an advertising service for businesses wanting to display ads on Google and its advertising network. The AdWords program enables businesses and marketing professionals to set a budget for online advertising and only pay when consumers click on the ads, we'll talk more about this later!

Affiliate Marketing

Affiliate marketing is an online advertising model whereby companies pay compensation to other organizations/online publishers to generate traffic and leads to the company's products and services. The third party organizations are referred to as affiliates and the commission fees that they earn incentivize them to promote the company's products. This model is normally used in support of an overarching eCommerce strategy whereby a clear ROI can be demonstrated through conversion.

Agile Marketing

Agile marketing, sometimes called always on marketing, refers to an approach and set of tactics that involve delivering marketing activity, on demand and subject to change and flexibility. Agile marketing is normally completed using sprints to complete high value activity in a short space of time, continuously improving results and helping to achieve rapid success. When working in an agile environment is it important to work as a team, track project success on progress boards, have daily standup meetings, sometimes held in a 'war-room' to help ensure activity is completed on time and in budget.

Alexa

Developed by internet giant Amazon Alexa is a voice activated intelligent personal assistant that sits inside Amazon Echo and Echo Dot devices. Alexa's capabilities replicate those of other artificial intelligent assistance such as Siri, Google Assistant and Microsoft Cortana. Alexa responds to voice control by providing information on products, music, news, weather, sport, entertainment and whole host more. The back-end technology that runs Alexa sits on Amazon Web Services in the cloud, this enables Alexa to understand and learn a user's preferences and expand functionality over time.

Algorithm

In its most basic form an algorithm is the process of solving a problem. When it comes to digital marketing it is important to know that platforms like Google and Facebook are built on literally hundreds of complex algorithms that help determine the outcome of things such as Google search and Facebook's timeline. Whilst it is near impossible to know and understand all of the algorithms that exist it is important to understand significant changes in these algorithms and how they may impact your marketing activity.

Alt Text

Alt text, or alternative text as it is also known is used within HTML code to describe the appearance and function of a particular image on a page. This is of specific importance from an SEO perspective on a website, ensuring all your alt text contains relevant keywords will really help!

Analytics

When it comes to digital marketing analytics typically involves the studying of past historical data to identify potential trends, to analyze the effects of certain decisions, or to evaluate the performance of a particular tool or scenario. The ultimate goal of analytics is to improve the overall performance of activity by using data to drive change. Analytics are a key component to pretty much every element of digital marketing, whether it be social media, CRM, digital media or website analysis. One final note is that there are numerous tools on the market to support you with analytics, make sure to do proper research and identify the tool that is most relevant to your specific activity.

Anchor Text

Anchor text is the clickable text contained within a hyperlink on a website. As part of your SEO strategy you should look to optimize anchor text across your website, best practice is to ensure that anchor text is relevant to the content on the page that you are linking to, ensuring you use relevant keywords will also help improve your overall ranking.

Application Programming Interface (API)

An API is a software intermediary that allows multiple applications to speak with one another. A great example of this is with smartphones. When you use an application on your mobile phone, the application connects to the internet and sends data back and forth, performing relevant actions. The data is then represented on your mobile device. The technology used to do this is known as API.

Artificial Intelligence (AI)

If anyone has seen the movie iRobot with Will Smith they should have some idea of AI. However, artificial intelligence doesn't have to reside in a human like robot. AI is actually the simulation of human intelligence processed by machines. AI can be used to perform tasks such as data analysis, in some cases more accurately and more efficiently than humans, enabling organizations to be more agile and gain more insights, quicker.

Attribution Model

Attribution modelling in digital media terms helps you to determine how you can credit a particular action, or lead, across multiple campaigns and touch points. In order to support this an attribution model needs to be built based on an overall consumer journey, typically from first touch/awareness through to conversion. Understanding an attribution model will help you to see which campaigns or marketing activity has contributed most to an overall outcome, data and analytics are key!

Augmented Reality (AR)

When people ask me to give them an example of AR I typically resort to the hotdog character created by Snapchat, nothing demonstrates this better! For those of you that weren't lucky enough to see this let me explain. AR is placement and integration of digital content in a user's environment, in real-time, typically delivered through a mobile device. Unlike VR, which I discuss later in this book, AR uses an existing, real, environment and overlays new content, typically used by brands to enhance a user's experience.

Avatar

In digital marketing terms an Avatar refers to a fictional character that represents an online user. These avatars are typically used in online gaming, chatrooms, online communities, web forums and even on social media. Avatars allow users to represent themselves online in whatever way they want, unlike using traditional profile photos, users can be as creative as their hearts desire.

B is for Bytes

Back End Development

There is often confusion when developing websites, applications etc regarding front and back end. Back end development refers to the server side of an application and everything that communicates between the database and the browser. Back end programming languages include the likes of Java, PHP and .Net, as well as a host of others. Typically, back end development and front end development should be joined at the hip. Front end ensuring good experience, back end ensuring logistically possible!

Backlinks

In its simplest form a backlink in an incoming hyperlink from one web page to another website. From an SEO perspective backlinks are very important and a major metric for the ranking of a website on Google and other search engines. When Google crawls websites it looks at the backlinks linking into a site, if a site has good quality links, i.e. links from other high-ranking sites, Google will use this information to help move the site up the rankings. Remember though, it is quality over quantity. A larger number of low quality, or false links could mean you get penalized!

Banner Ads

A banner ad, or web banner is essentially an image-based form of website advertising, as opposed to the text based PPC format. These adverts are delivered through an ad server and are embedded on various different webpages. The goal of these banner ads, simple, generate awareness and drive traffic through to another website/webpage. Banner ads come in a number of different shapes and sizes including small square, square, banner, leaderboard and skyscraper.

Beta

So I could be wrong but I think Beta actually comes from the reek alphabet, but don't quote me on that. Inn digital terms the word beta actually refers to a product, typically a website, that is ready for pre-release testing, usually by a controlled group of users in real life work situations. For example, if you are building a new website you would typically test in-house first, this would be referred to as alpha testing, then when you are ready to push live you would 'beta test' with a controlled number of customers, sometimes called a soft launch, before final changes and 'go-live'.

Bid Management

Bid management involves the automated management of bidding for digital marketing campaigns. Bid management tools, also known as bid optimization platforms, enable you to automate your cost-per-click bids across different campaigns. Real time bidding (RTB) is an automated auction for the purchase of individual ad impressions on websites and other digital assets. RTB is a core component of programmatic advertising, which essentially automates the processes and transactions involved in buying and placing your ads.

Big Data

Big data is a marketing term that has been thrown around for many years now, along with data is king! Big data is typically used to describe a massive volume of both structured and unstructured data that is so large it is difficult to manage and process using traditional databases. With regards to digital marketing big data has the potential to help companies improve marketing activity and make faster, more intelligent decisions based on data and insights. Typically data is collected from a number of sources including emails, mobile devices, applications, databases, websites, servers and social media. This data is then captured, formatted, manipulated, and then analyzed!

Bitly

Bitly is actually a service that enables users to shorten URLs. This type of service is typically used on social media and on platforms such as instant messaging, basically anywhere where a limited number of characters are required. Put simply

Bitly takes long URLs and replaces the entire URL link with a shorter series of numbers and letters, ultimately saving space.

Black hat

The term black hat actually has a two main meanings, neither very positive. The first use of black hat refers to a computer hacker who breaks into a network or computer systems with malicious intent. The second refers to its use in SEO. Black hat SEO refers to a set of negative practices that are used to increase a site or page's ranking within search engines through means that essentially violate best practices and a search engines' term of service. Most search engines are now smart to this type of malpractice and have algorithms in place to detect and penalize websites that follow these practices.

Blockchain

When many people ask me what Blockchain is I answer simply, the future! Blockchain a lot like cryptocurrency is peer-to-peer and is a type of ledger for maintaining a record of transactional data, permanently and without risk of tampering or fraud. Blcokchain is being explored by a number of different industry sectors as a secure and cost effective way to create and manage distributed data and maintain records for digital transactions of all types.

Blog

The text book answer to this is a website or webpage that is often run by just one individual, or a small group. Typically, blogs are updated on a regular basis and written in an informal conversation style. Blogs are often based around a specialist subject, for example 'cooking blog', 'travel blog' etc and contain an individual's personal reflections, comments and often content such as video and images. To see an example of a great blog feel free to check out mine: www.the-digital-diary.com

Blogger

A blogger is essentially the individual who writes and owns a blog or regularly writes material for a blog. As a brand it is important to build solid relationships with relevant bloggers. Bloggers can do a fantastic job of amplifying your message, especially as print publication numbers continue to drop. As consumers more of us are turning to specialist bloggers for news and information, particularly around specialist topics. Many bloggers tend to take an impartial view on subjects so their opinion and voice can drive real impact for brands.

Blogosphere

Love this term! The blogosphere is best described as the social universe created by online individuals (bloggers) using website publishing platforms (blogs). In other words the blogosphere describes all the blogs on the internet! With this in mind the blogosphere is very diverse, and very difficult to control, as it contains views, opinions, thoughts, facts and fiction posted by bloggers from all corners of the world!

Bookmarking

Growing up as a child I used bookmarks to put between the pages of my books so that I could pick up my reading where I left off with ease, bookmarking in a digital sense works in exactly the same way. A bookmark is essentially a saved shortcut that directs a user's browser directly to a specific webpage. Saving bookmarks allows users to easily access their favourite websites at the click of a button, improving time navigating around the web and improving overall user experience.

Bounce Rate

One of my favourite metrics! Bounce rate is typically used in website analytics to measure the number of people who navigate away from a site after viewing only one page. This is one of the metrics that you need to drive as low as possible, from a bench mark perspective you should look to get your bounce rate under 30%

Browser

A web browser is the interface we all use to display HTML files and navigate the world wide web. The most popular browsers used today include Chrome, Safari and Internet Explorer. It is important when developing web applications that you test across all browsers as you want to ensure the experience for consumers is the same, regardless of what browser they are using.

Business Intelligence (BI)

Business Intelligence, or BI as it is also know, is used to help marketers and business leaders make better business decisions. BI refers specifically to technology, applications and practices for the mining, integration, analysis and presentation of data and information. There are many number of BI tools available on the market that can be used to help visualize data and these have become the standard over the past few years thanks to digital marketing and the vast amounts of data that exist. With the trend of 'big data' BI tools are increasingly being used as front end interfaces for big data systems, allowing a unified view of divers data that would take hours and hours to analyze by an individual.

C is for Computer

Cache

In digital marketing terms a cache is a place used to store temporary files and active data. Typically when browsing on websites data is cached to reduce latency and time to load in future visits.

Chat Rooms

Chat rooms are areas of websites or places on a computer network where users can communicate with each other about a specific project. Typically these are housed in forums and group pages and allow users the ability to converse with multiple people in the same conversation at the same time.

Chatbots

Chatbots are computer programs that are designed to simulate conversation with users, typically a service-based application powered by complex rules and algorithms and in some cases artificial intelligence that allows users to interact and engage in one-to-one conversation. Chatbots are being used more and more as a form of customer service, especially out of hours, ensuring that consumers always have 'someone' to speak to and log their queries/complaints.

Clickability

The word clickability describes the degree of desirability and functionality that a link is on a webpage. Links with high clickability are attractive to the eye (beauty is in the eye of the beholder) and have a distinct call-to-action.

Clickbait

Clickbait is eye-catching content that is pushed out on a website, often social media platforms, that encourages users to click on a link to drive to a specific site. We often find that clickbait imagery and headlines aim to exploit a particular curiosity gap, providing just enough information to make a user curious enough to click!

Click Through Rate (CTR)

CTR is a metric used to measure the success of a particular online ad. The exact formula used is number of clicks that you ad receives divided by the number of times your ad is shown. CTR doesn't have to be restricted to online ads, you can also measure the CTR on a webpage or an email campaign. Achieving a high CTR should always be your goal and there are various things you can do to test and learn how to improve this number of time.

Cloud

The term Cloud can be used to describe specific online services which are collectively labeled as cloud computing. Examples of popular cloud-based services include web applications, online back-up, web hosting, email and online gaming. Social networking websites such as Facebook are also cloud-based services as the information of yours that is on them is stored online. The word cloud was considered a buzzword for many years. however, its application today is vast, helping to store and share content and information for both consumers and businesses alike.

Community Management

The truth is that the definition of community management is likely to differ from organization to organization. For me community management is about building and sustaining an emotional connection with consumers, typically over social media. In the agencies I have run we have had teams of 'community managers' working on behalf of clients, their job to communicate in real time with our clients end customers on social media. The end goal of these community managers to create and manage an online community where people feel that they belong, and their voices are heard.

Content Management Systems (CMS)

A CMS system is basically a software based application that is used to create and manage digital content. CMS systems/platforms are typically the bedrock of any good website and they help to manage and facilitate collaboration and integrated working by allowing multiple users to create and publish content online. There are a number of different CMS solutions available from free online applications to high end enterprise alternatives. Some of the most popular include WordPress, Drupal, Joomla!, Radiant and Sitecore.

Content Marketing

How many times have you heard the phrase 'content is king'? It goes without saying that in today's modern-day age where the consumer is becoming more and more savvy content marketing is more important than ever. In digital marketing terms content marketing involves the creation and sharing of online material/content, such as videos, blogs, social media posts, images etc. Typically this content does not promote or advertise a brand like typical advertisements but is designed to stimulate interest and build engagement with a target audience.

Contextual Advertising

Contextual advertising is all about relevancy, typically ads are served on page where the content is relevant to the advertisement. One of the best know examples off contextual advertising is Google AdSense where Google robots automatically serve ads that are deemed relevant to your users. Contextual advertising can take make forms, such as in-game advertising, Video advertising and native advertising.

Contextual Search

Contextual search is a form of optimized search results based on understanding the context with which the user was searching, essentially returning answers or a list of answers that is optimized based on relevancy of context. This increased precision ensures that results are shown and based on how valuable they are to the user.

Conversion Rate Optimization (CRO)

In digital marketing terms conversion rate optimization is essentially a system for increasing the percentage of visitors to a website that convert to customers, or complete the desired action or goal on a webpage. CRO is of particular benefit when optimizing lower funnel media activity as part of an eCommerce strategy. Whilst top of funnel activity would typically focus on general brand awareness lower funnel activity needs to be more fine-tuned to ensure an optimal conversion rate.

Cookie

Cookies come in many different varieties, chocolate chip, fruit and nut….on a serious note this isn't a cook book! In digital terms a cookie is a small amount of data that is generated by a website and saved in your browser. The purpose of this data is to remember information about you and improve your experience on certain sites when you return, for example having certain fields pre-filled, such as username and passwords, based on your previous interactions.

Cost-Per-Click (CPC)

CPC refers to the actual price that you pay for each and every click in your pay-per-click marketing campaign. When you setup a campaign in AdWords you will need to set a maximum cost-per-click bid, this is the highest amount that you are willing to pay for a click on your advert.

Cost-Per-Customer (CPC/CAC)

Cost-Per-Customer is also known as Customer-Acquisition-Cost. The CAC means the price you pay to acquire a new customer. It is typically based on a very simple calculation, dividing the total cost associated with acquisition by total number of new customers within a specific timeframe.

Cost-Per-Lead (CPL)

CPL actually refers to a pricing model specifically designed to support online advertising. In this model the advertiser pays for a sign-up from an end consumer interested in the advertisers offer. Applying a CPL model ensures that advertisers only pay for qualified conversions, typically you would use this model if you are looking to sign-up consumers or maybe as part of an app download program, enabling you to generate a guaranteed return on marketing investment.

Cost-Per-Thousand (CPM)

CPM is an online advertising model that refers to advertising space being bought on the bases of impressions. Impressions are typically sold per thousand on a particular webpage. For example, if you a website publisher charges a CPM of $1.50, that means that the advertiser must pay $1.50 for every 1,000 impressions of its ad. This type of advertising is typically used at top of funnel brand awareness level.

Cross-Device

The term cross device can be summarized by then involvement of multi screens, including laptops, tablets, phones, desktop computers and even televisions. Marketers often try to find out when their messages reach consumers on different devices throughout the day, identifying users accurately as they switch screens. Cross-device data lets marketers avoid repeating messages to the same person on different screens more than they want to.

Crowdfunding

Crowdfunding is a methodology and process of funding a specific project or business venture by raising money online from large number of different people who essentially each contribute a relatively small amount. Crowdfunding uses social media and crowdfunding websites to reach large numbers of investors and entrepreneurs and bring them together to raise money.

Crowdsourcing

The term crowdsourcing is a combination of the words crowd and outsourcing and describes the practice of turning to a body of people to obtain information, knowledge, goods or services. Whether an individual or an organization requests specific resources from a group of people, the crowd, they are seen to be crowdsourcing. There are a number of platforms on the internet and social media that can used to help support the process of crowdsourcing.

Cryptocurrency

This a hot topic right now, every time I turn my laptop on I am seeing ads for Bitcoin and other cryptocurrencies. Cryptocurrencies are essentially a digital or virtual currency whereby a number of encryption techniques are used to regulate and verify the transfer of funds.

CSS

CSS or cascading style sheets as they are also known are used to format the layout of web pages on a website. CSS is used to define text styles and other elements of a web page that helps developers create a uniform look across multiple pages.

Curator

A content creator in marketing terms is someone who finds, groups, organizes and shares relevant content on a specific topic online. As a brand curating someone else's content, having an opinion, particularly on social media, can be a great way to gain exposure and raise awareness. If you want to position yourself as an expert in your field whilst creating your own content is of high importance, curating existing content can be a quicker and cheaper way to amplify your credentials.

Customer Experience (CX)

Ultimately customer experience is defined by the perception a customer has of your brand. However, understanding a consumers experience with your brand or organization from a physical and emotional perspective can help you to drive a positive outcome. Typically, this would be done through customer journey mapping to help identify moments that matter and how you as a brand can add value to a consumer's life, helping to build that perception and overall experience.

Customer Relationship Management (CRM)

CRM refers to processes, technologies, strategies, people and overall practices that companies use to analyze and manage customer interactions, usually data driven, across an entire customer lifecycle and relationship with a brand. The ultimate goal of CRM is to build and improve business relationships with customers to ensure customer satisfaction and overall business growth. From a digital perspective the art of CRM is building these relationships through one to one communications cross multiple digital touchpoints including websites, email and social media.

D is for Data

Data

Writing about data could very much be a chapter on its own –
this is a huge topic! In its simplest form data is information.
Data typically falls into two categories, structured and
unstructured. Structured data is basic and easily searchable;
spreadsheets are a great example. Unstructured data is
slightly more complex and less 'rule based', typically text-
heavy but may also contain numbers as well. Due to the
growth of the internet and content creation data storage
measurements have grown considerably over time.

Database

In its simplest for a database is a data structure that stores
organized information, data! Databases typically contain data
that is stored in tables and fields, think of a giant excel
spreadsheet. From a digital marketing perspective it is
important to understand that eCommerce sites use databases
to store product inventory and customer information. These
sites will normally use a database management system, such
as Access or MySQL as the back-end to the website. The key
factor to using a database is ease of use. When data is stored
in a database it can be very easily searched, sorted and

updated. This flexibility is of key importance for eCommerce sites.

Deep Linking

A deep link is essentially a hyperlink on the internet that drives a user to a page on another website other than its homepage. The word 'deep' refers to the depth of the page in the sites structure of pages.

Deterministic

Deterministic is data that can accurately identify a consumer for targeting ads., such as visitors login information for a website. Other deterministic data points include phone numbers, credit card details and addresses.

Digital Content

Digital content, digital media, comes in many different forms, text, audio, video, images and animation for example. In most cases digital content refers specifically to content that can be downloaded or distributed across the internet or devices such as eReaders and smart phones. Pretty much any type of content that you are looking at, watching or reading on the internet is classed as digital content.

Digital Transformation (DT)

Digital transformation is essentially the change of an organization in line with the application of digital technology across all aspects of an organization. Typically this transformation leads to the adoption of new innovative technology to enhance and upgrade traditional processes and methodology.

Direct Messaging

Thanks to social media direct messaging has become the norm! As consumers we are able to send direct messages to each other on multiple platforms, Facebook, IG, Titter etc. This being developed now so that we can send direct messages to multiple users by way of creating intimate groups. More importantly direct messaging means that brands are able to build one to one relationships through these personal communications, allowing consumers to reach brans with problems and complaints and brands to reach consumers with personalized promotions and deals.

Display Advertising

Display advertising is another name for banner ads. Unlike text based PPC ads on search engines display advertising can incorporate text, logos, pictures, images, even video! The main purpose of display advertising is to generate awareness and ultimately drive traffic to a destination website.

DMP

DMP stands for Data Management Platform. In digital marketing terms DMPs essentially have two main meanings. The first from of DMP is in relation to display advertising where a data management platform is used to manage data associated with ad impressions and is used by ad networks, ad exchanges and publishers. The second form of DMPs refers to enterprise data management and is dedicated to manage all kinds of touch points, often called Enterprise DMPs.

DNS

This is where we get a little techie! The DNS or domain name system, is the way the internet domain names are located and translated in IP addresses. Web browsers rely on DNS to quickly provide information to enable a swift connection between user and websites.

Domain Name

A domain name is a unique name that essentially identifies a website. For example the domain name of Facebook is Facebook.com. The domain name always appears in the address bar of a web browser and can be used to drive a consumer directly to a website. When building a website it is important to register a domain name through an online registration portal such as Go-Daddy. The problem is that as internet usage grows the number of available domain names is becoming smaller and smaller.

DSP

DSP actually refers to Demand Side Platform, a tech platform that gives media buyers access to ad exchanges and ad networks in an RTB environment. A DSP is connected with multiple sources of ad inventory that allows buyers to bid for single ad impressions according to targeting and price restrictions and well defined goals, ultimately allowing media buyers to bid on display, video, social and mobile ads.

E is for Email

Earned Media

Earned media, or free media as it is also known, refers to publicity gained through promotional efforts other than paid media advertising., which refers to publicity gained through advertising, or owned media, which refers to owned assets and branding. Traditionally earned media has been the role of PR. However, with the explosion of social media and influencers, earned media should be something that is considered as part of your digital strategy. Earned influence involves leveraging influencers to help amplify your message.

eBook

As we continue to digitalize and print slowly deceases we are seeing a huge surge in eBooks. In summary an eBook is an electronic version of a traditional print book that is typically read using an eBook reader like a Kindle. eBooks are typically cheaper that traditional print-based alternatives and due to the digitalization consumers are now able to transport entire book collections on a single device!

eCommerce

eCommerce refers to business transactions, particularly sale lead, over the internet, that's online shopping to you and me! There are essentially two different types of ecommerce, business-to-business and business-to-consumer, the later referring to sites like Amazon, eBay etc and the process of shopping for personal products. When looking at an overall eCommerce strategy it is important to look at every aspect of the process, including upfront media and lead generation, instore experience, pricing and promotion strategy and back end fulfilment and delivery!

EdTech

EdTech is a term used to describe Educational Technology and software. Typically, this software is designed to enhance teacher-led learning in classrooms and improve the overall learning outcome of student education. Like MarTech and FinTech, EdTech describes a new way of working that is often supported by digital technology such as artificial intelligence.

Email Marketing

Email marketing for those of you that have been living on another planet for the past 25 years is the sending of communication from one user to another, using email. Email marketing on mass can be a great way to communicate with customers and up-sell/cross sell additional products and services, it can also be used as an acquisition tool to new prospects. Either way email marketing should form an integral part of your digital strategy.

Emoji

According to the Oxford English Dictionary an Emoji is best described as a small digital image or icon used to express an idea or emotion. Due to the quick adoption of Emoji's, largely driven through mobile application, there is even an Emoji dictionary that exists to help old folk like me understand the true meaning behind your favourite smileys!

Employee Amplification

Employee amplification is a term used to describe the amplification of a particular message or news through employees. Typically this is done using social media channels and digital communication.

Engagement Rate

Engagement rate is a metric that is commonly used to measure the success of a piece of content created, usually published on social channels. Engagement rate shows how much consumers have interacted with the content. Typical factors that are used to measure engagement include likes, comments, shares and reactions.

Expandable Banners

A banner ad that can expand to a larger size when a user hovers their mouse cursor over the banner or when they click on it.

F is for Facebook

Facebook

I couldn't do an A-Z of digital marketing without including Facebook! The most popular social media platform on the planet Facebook is available in over 37 languages, has over 2 billion users and has completely transformed how we communicate online. For any business have a presence on Facebook should be a key part of your digital marketing strategy.

Facebook Live

Facebook Live is a feature on Facebook that allows users and businesses to offer live-streaming of video content to other users, fans and followers. This technique has been heavily adopted by the media who use this to report on events in real-time. Consumers today have a thirst for real-time live content, marketing and brand engagement, tools like Facebook Live are a great way to build this engagement.

Facebook Pixel

A Facebook Pixel is a piece of code that is applied to a website. As with other pixels a Facebook pixel allows you to track traffic and conversions from advertisements that are placed on Facebook. This gives you the opportunity to optimize ads based on data collected, build targeted audience groups for future advertising campaigns and remarket to qualified leads.

Fans

A social media fan or follower is a user who likes a particular page or account. These fans are then able to receive updates from that page's administrator through content being published such as posts and tweets. These users are essentially your warm leads a these are people who have raised their hand to say that they are a fan/follower of your products and services, offering them rewards is a great way to buying advocacy.

Favicon

A favicon is a small icon that is used to identify a website in a web browser. Most websites display the Favicon of a website just to the left hand side of the address bar, next to the URL. Whilst A Favicon is probably one of the smallest elements to consider when developing a website from a branding and consistency perspective they are key!

FinTech

The term FinTech refers to financial technology, largely changing the financial industry today. The best example of FinTech at the moment is probably Blockchain and cryptocurrencies. However, as financial services organizations have always been at the forefront of digital FinTech could be used to describe any type of technology that helps to enable and improve financial based processes.

Firewall

A firewall is a network security system that can be either hardware of software based. The main purpose of a firewall is to control incoming and outgoing network traffic to prevent security breaches and ensure that unauthorized access to sensitive information is blocked.

Floating Ad

A floating ad is a type of rich media advertisement that appears uninitiated, superimposed, over a specific web-page. These ads normally disappear after a short period of time. The most basic floating ads appear over a web page, either full screen or in a smaller rectangular window, they normally provide a means of escape such as a close button. Utilizing Flash and dynamic HTML you can create floating ads of any shape, size and even include interactive components such as sound and animation. Floating Ads do a great job of grabbing a user's attention and tend to be more interesting than traditional ads, often generating a much higher click-through rate and number of impressions.

Forums

A forum, in digital marketing terms, is a section of a website that allows users to communicate with each other in a group-based format using messages. Forums are usually setup around specific topics to ensure that users are able to converse with each other around a particular thread. Forums can add great value to a website from an SEO perspective as the content that is created is user generated, often when filtering through search results on a search engine you will notice forum based content ranking well.

Freemium

The word freemium is typically used to describe a pricing strategy in which the basic version of the service or product is offered free of charge. Extra features and functionality requires users to upgrade to paid versions. This strategy is heavily used with mobile applications and is a great way to get consumers to try an app before making a purchase.

Frequency

Frequency is a term often used in display advertising and refers to the number of times your ads are seen by a particular person. Frequency marketing on the other hand is a strategy used to communicate with a particular audience over a long period of time, sometimes used as part of lead nurturing for longer sales cycles.

Front End Development

Front end development refers to the programming of the front end of a website including creating of the visual elements to a website. This includes creating components and features that are directly viewed and accessed by the end user. Front end development will typically bridge the gap between creative design and back end development, taking raw design files and converting them into HTML, javascript and CSS code.

FTP

An FTP is a standard network protocol used for the transfer of computer files between a client and server on a computer network. An FTP is normally protected with a username and password to protect files, programs and information and limit access.

G is for Google, of course!

Gamification

There is a common misconception when it comes to the term gamification, let me tell you what it is not, online games!!!! Gamification is actually the application of game theory concepts and techniques to non-game activities. The overall goal of gamification is to engage a user with an activity that they find fun in order to influence their behavior, typically used as part of the overall path to purchase. A gamification initiative should address the cognitive and emotional aspects of game theory as well as the social ones by including a system of rules for participants to explore through active experimentation and discovery, awarding points or badges for levels of participation, displaying leaderboards to encourage competition and even offering prizes so that consumers have the chance to actually win something.

Geotargeting

Geotargeting is the process of delivering content to a specific user or group of users based on their geographical location. The aim of geotargeting is to improve cost efficiencies of marketing programs by targeting relevant messaging to consumers within a certain vicinity. This can be very effective if you are trying to drive footfall to a particular location or have a promotion in a certain city and you want to capitalize on those who are nearest.

GIF

In its simplest format an animated GIF is a moving file that is created using multiple images or frames. These are then played when opened or displayed on a browser or social platform. The end result is a quirky animated clip or short movie. With the rise in popularity of social media and with brands wanting to cut through to their target audience GIFs are a great way at creating cheap visual content.

Google AMP

AMP stands for Accelerated Mobile Pages and this is a Google backed project designed to have web pages load quicker on mobile devices, ultimately improving the overall user experience on mobile devices.

Google Analytics (GA)

Its probably worth me stating that there are other analytics platforms available. However, it is fair to say that Google Analytics is the go-to analytics platform for most organisations. It is a free web analytics service that is offered by Google that tracks and reports website performance, traffic and overall user behavior on a specific website.

Google Assistant

Google assistant is Google's voice activated artificial intelligent assistant for android devices. Google assistant provides a virtual personal assistant experience through a natural language speech interface to perform a variety of tasks. As a voice assistant Google assistant adds two-way conversation abilities to Googles previous assistant service, Google Now., which was a web and text-based service. The latest version of Google assistant uses cognitive computing, machine learning and voice recognition technology. Other voice activated digital assistant technology on the market includes Siri and Alexa!

Google Display network (GDN)

GDN is a great way to reach your audience and build brand awareness by reaching your target market whilst they are browsing their favourite sites. There are a number of different ad types available on GDN including responsive, images (multi size), videos, engagement ads and even gmail based ads. You can then measure the performance of your campaigns using AdWords.

Google Home

Google Home is Google's answer to Amazon Echo, and uses its own AI, Google Assistant, very similar to Alexa. Google Home is a Wi-Fi speaker that doubles as a smart home control centre and digital PA for the family and home! Google Home can be used to play entertainment like music and can even be wired into your television providing voice active viewing. You can ask Google literally anything, news, sports results, weather reports, it can also be synced up to your gmail account and calendar.

Google Plus

Google Plus is a social networking platform owned and operated by Google. Whilst initial pick-up of Google plus was strong the numbers have declined. There are some unique features to Google Plus such as Hangouts, Circles, Streams, Sparks and Huddles! One of the key USPs of Google Plus is its integration with other platforms such as Gmail, Google Drive, Google Maps and even Google Calendar.

H is for Hard drive

H2H Marketing

Human to human marketing is an approach to marketing whereby brands try to create an authentic connection between a brand and their consumers. H2H marketing is best described as the process of building empathetic relationships, rather than traditional transaction based relationships. Essentially to truly perform H2H marketing a brand must understand their customer, their needs, requirements, pain points and build a long lasting value add relationship.

Hashing

Hashing is a way to hide personal information when it is shared between ad-tech partners. For example, if a brand asks a publisher to target ads to its customer list, the emails can be masked, kind of like translating them into a different language that only the computer will be able to read.

#Hashtag

Hashtags are used on social media platforms, especially on Twitter and Instagram, to help identify messages or specific topics. Using hashtags helps users to find content based on search queries, they can also be an integral part of branding and online activity such as competitions. Developing a hashtag strategy should be a key part of your overall social media plans.

Header Image

A header image, or hero image, as it is sometimes known is the main image at the top of a traditionally laid out website design. Typically brands use this space for advertising particular promotions, deals, events etc. In many cases these header images can be part of a carousel to help drive multiple promotions. As these images are typically the first thing that you see on a website it is essential that the image and copy are of high quality and encourage the user to click for more information.

Home Page

In its simplest for a home page is the first and main page of a website. The home page usually contains links to other pages within the site and is a good place to advertise promotions and particular products and services. Whilst consumers can enter a site via any page more often than not this is their first port of call and landing page, ensuring the content is up-to-date and informs the consumer about your business and brand is key.

Homepage Takeover

A homepage takeover is a display advert that involves a single creative appearing all over a sites homepage. This gives an advertiser 100% share of voice on the homepage as no other ads are normally shown. It is probably of no surprise that these are classed as a 'premium buy', they are sold on a CPM basis and can cost over $250,000 per ad! Due to their expensive nature they are usually used for branding campaigns or to support particular product launches and events.

Hosting

Hosting is the terminology used to describe the housing, serving and maintenance files associated with a websites. Typically organisations use hosting services provided by third party organsiations who also provide additional support and SLAs. Hosting packages can be bought in a number of different sizes to help support different sized websites and different bandwidth requirements.

HTML

HTML is a set of code and symbols that are inserted into a file that is used as part of a website. This code tells the web browser how to display the content on the web page, such as text and imagery. Each piece of code referring back to an individual element of the webpage. Typically this is the first phase of website development post creative input and before back end development.

Hyperlink

A hyperlink is an element of a website, email or electronic document, that links to another page in either the same document or to an entirely different location. Typically, a user clicks on the hyperlink to follow the link to the new location. These are an essential element to any website to help reduce bounce rate and encourage users on a path to purchase or to drive consumers to new content.

Hyperlocal

Hyperlocal advertising is typically used when pushing out mobile ads via a user's smartphone. Utilizing location based data hyperlocal ads are served to people that fall within a particular geographical radius. Most buying platforms have either a mapping integration built-in, or allow you to upload a list of GPS coordinates what you want to target. This form of advertising is perfect if you are looking to drive footfall to a particular on ground event, shop or restaurant, ensuring you reach people within the vicinity!

I is for iPhone

Ideation

The term ideation best describes the creative process of generating, developing and communicating new creative ideas. Ideation today should include digital and innovation at the core.

Impressions

Impressions are when an online ad or any other form of digital media is presented on a user's screen. An impression is defined by a user potentially seeing the ad, making CPM based media campaigns an ideal approach if you are looking to build awareness and ensure your ads are seen by as many people as possible.

Inbound Marketing

Inbound marketing is a concept and strategy that focusses on helping brands to attract potential consumers to come to them through content-based marketing. Typically, this approach is used in B2B marketing or where an organization is looking to drive inbound sales leads that could potentially then be contacted and qualified further by the advertising organization.

Influencer

An influencer, or KOL as they are also known is a person that has the ability to influencer the behavior or opinions of others online, typically their followers. One of the most well-known online influencers has to be Kim Kardashian who has millions of followers across her multiple social media platforms. Brands typically work with influencers by paying them to endorse their products or services online to their fan base, helping to drive awareness and conversion.

Influencer Relationship Management (IRM)

Influencer relationship management best describes the strategy of managing influencers interactions, inspired by Customer Relationship Management. Setting up an IRM program as part of your overall social strategy is a key part of digital today. An IRM strategy will help you to identify the perfect blend of influencers for your brand, ensuring maximum reach, awareness and engagement. The key is then the ongoing management and analysis of the influencer performance to enable you to make changes over the course of the activity.

Infographic

An infographic is a representation of information and content in a graphic format, ultimately designed to make the data easily understandable at a glance and often highly shareable. Brands use infographics to quickly communicate a message and simplify the presentation of large amounts of information. Brands typically use infographics in a B2B environment, they provide great visual content for platforms such as LinkedIn and done correctly can be highly valuable and shareable. A great way to amplify your message!

Instagram

Instagram for those of you that do not know is one of the fastest growing social media platforms. Instagram is an online image and video sharing platform that was acquired by Facebook in 2012. Instagram has changed photography and enabled every one of us to be creative through their online editing tools on the application.

Instagram Stories

IG stories is one of the latest features on Instagram that enables users and brands to post images and videos that will then vanish after 24 hours. This feature was originally the backbone of the social platform Snapchat. With the rise in live content this is a great tool to enable brands to run promotions and report on live events. Furthermore the number of brands using this is still quite low, enabling great cut through and penetration.

Instant Messaging (IM)

Instant messaging is defined by the sending and receiving of real-time messages via a stand-alone application. There are a number of IM applications available today including Facebook messenger, Gmail, Skype and of course WhatsApp messenger. Instant messaging has replaced the use of SMS and created the birth of the Emoji ☺

Interstitial

Interstitial best describes an ad that pops up while a user is clicking to a new page online. An interstitial can take over the homepage on a website or occupy the whole screen when someone click on a link in an app and opens the mobile web. Most of these types of ads have been flagged by companies like Google as too disruptive of the user experience, and websites that use them may face penalties in search rankings!

Intranet

An intranet is private restricted website and network, typically used to house company information within an organization. A company intranet is usually used to house internal communication, for example employee related information such as a directory.

IP Address

An IP address is a unique set of numbers that are separated by full stops. These numbers are used to identify each computer using the internet. IP addresses can be used as part of digital marketing activity to help with targeting. For geo-based campaigns IP targeting can drive fantastic results!

ISP

ISP stands for internet service provider and is a company that provides individuals and organizations with access to the internet. ISPs provide end consumers the ability to communicate with each other through online email accounts, telephone and television based services.

J is for James Gaubert

Javascript (JS)

Javascript is the language used on the internet to enhance HTML code and pages. HTML pages are great for displaying static content. However, many websites today have varying degrees of functionality including menus, images, video, forms etc. Javascript is the language used by programmer and developers to bring these elements to life and create an interactive online experience.

JPEG/JPG

Quite simply a JPEG is an image file! This is the most common image file type not only used by computers but also other devices like digital cameras.

Junk Mail

Junk email, or spam as it is more commonly known, refers to unwanted or unsolicited email communications, typically in the form of advertising or the promotion of material that has not been requested.

K is for Keynote

Keywords

Keywords are the essence of any content being used on a website and form a key element to an SEO strategy. They are also one of the most important factors when looking to build a paid media campaign on Google search. Whether you are building a website or creating ads to drive consumers to a website you need to ensure that the keywords that you use are relevant to what people are searching for.

Keyword research

Detailed keyword research is an important practice that applies to both SEO and PPC related professionals and campaigns/activity. This process involves the detailed studying of consumer behavior to identify insights and keywords and terms that users use when searching on search engines that tie back to a brands products and services. These keywords should then be used in ad copy and website content to help drive consumers to content that answers their search queries.

L is for Likes

Landing page

A landing page is one of those terms that has multiple meaning. In one instance a landing page can refer to a web page which serves as the entry point for a website or a particular section of a website, in some cases simple 'landing pages' are setup to support specific campaigns, events or activity, like a microsite.

Likes

In social media terms a like is one of the measurements used to analyze the performance of a particular piece of content. Users are able to show their appreciation for content on social media by hitting the 'like button'. In the early days of social media this was a key metric. However, as social continues to develop and mature the value of likes has been questioned.

LinkedIn

LinkedIn is a social media platform specifically designed to support the business community. Unlike other social platforms the main role of LinkedIn is to allow users the ability to share professional work related content with other users and online professionals. LinkedIn has also really picked up with business use, especially as a recruitment and lead generation tool.

Link Juice

The term link juice is an SEO based term that refers to how powerful a certain link is or could be. A link from a well-established, well known and well trusted site will pass more 'juice' than one on a pointless directory. From a Google perspective, when looking at an SEO backlink strategy, you are better to focus your efforts on a smaller number of quality links than a higher volume of low quality links.

Live streaming

Live streaming refers to the online streaming of content and the broadcast of material in real-time to users. Streaming can be used for a number of topics such as social content, online gaming, news broadcasting and television. In today's modern digital world consumers have a greater thirst for live content, especially as a news and PR channel. Brands have been quick to adopt this technology to interact with consumers in real-time, ensuring that no matter where a consumer lives they are able to be at events and see what is going on live!

Lookalike Targeting

Lookalike targeting is a digital marketing technique which involves reaching out to an audience similar to your existing customers. This form of advertising is typically used as part of a customer acquisition program and will help you to reach a new audience. Facebook as a specific lookalike targeting element called Lookalike Audiences which is a great way to profile existing followers and help you identify new ones!

Long tail keywords

Long tail keywords should form an important part to your SEO strategy. These are defined and search phrases that contain at least three words. Typically long tail keywords should be used to target very niche topics rather than a mass audience. The key to driving good quality traffic to your website is relevance and whilst long tail keywords may drive greater relevancy the volumes may not be as high as shorter generic keywords.

Lost Impression Share

Lost impression share (budget) is the percent of impressions an ad lost out on because of an insufficient budget. Lost impression share (rank) is the percent of impressions an ad lost out on because of a low ad rank. Impression share is used to evaluate the marketplace opportunity (or customer demand) for a defined set of keywords. Impression share is meant to answer the question 'How often is my ad served when consumers are searching my keywords?'

M is for Microsoft

Mailing list

A mailing list is an integral part of any digital marketer's toolset. Essentially a mailing list contains a list of contact details, including name, email address etc of people who have subscribed to a particular communication, a newsletter for example.

Mail Server

A mail server is a system that enables the sending and receiving of emails. Email servers typically use standard email protocols such as SMTP for sending emails and IMAP and POP3 for receiving emails and processing massages.

Marketing Automation

Marketing automation describes the use of technology and software to automate marketing processes such as customer acquisition, data integration and campaign management. The use of marketing automation makes processes that would otherwise have been performed manually much more efficient, and makes some new processes possible. Marketing automation can help you to streamline efficiency=ies, time and ensure your marketing activity is as accurate as possible, it also performs an integral part of an agile strategy.

MarTech

MarTech is best described as the blending of marketing and technology. Today pretty much anyone who works in digital marketing is working with MarTech. Then term MarTech is typically used when describing enterprise projects within an organization where process and technology is being implemented and used to help achieve improved marketing related goals and objectives. When looking at specific tools to support MarTech your stack may well include programmatic ad platforms, marketing automation software, content management systems, web analytics tools, CRM systems and even digital customer experience platforms.

Mash-up

In digital marketing terms a mash-up can be described as a web page or application that integrates elements from two or more sources and presents the results through an interface.

mCommerce

mCommerce, or mobile commerce as it is also known, describes the process of buying and selling products and services through a wireless device like a smartphone. As our lives continue to revolve around our mobile devices this is fast becoming the preferred method of choice for online shoppers, particular those who are on the go!

Meme

If you were born anytime post 1990 you should know exactly what a meme is but did you know that the word Meme actually comes from the Greek work 'mimema'; meaning something that is imitated? In digital terms a meme is something such as an image, phrase or video that is typically shared on social media platforms, often funny and with high virality.

Mention

The word mention in this instance relates to social mentions. In summary a social mention occurs each time a keyword, brand or even hashtag that you are monitoring is used on social media. These are typically used to measure the sentiment or engagement levels associated with the specific mention.

Metadata

Metatdata is often described as data about data....confused? In SEO terms the term metadata often refers to the content and context of information on a web page. Metadata is used to describe content on a website and provide this information to search engines to help indexing of your page and to drive relevant traffic to your site.

Metatag

A lot like metadata metatags are unseen markups/elements of code that are applied to a website and specifically web pages to help index web pages on search engines. Metatags are essentially little contend descriptors, ensuring these are optimized with the relevant keywords will help to drive qualified relevant organic traffic to your website.

Micro-Moments

Micro-moments is a term that has been coined by Google to describe the moment during a customer journey or path to purchase whereby a consumer turns to a device to act on a need – to know, go, do or buy! There are four key moments that truly matter and that you need to understand, these include, I want to know moments, when someone is exploring or researching, but is not in the purchase cycle. I want to go moments, when someone is looking for a local business or is considering buying a product at a nearby store. I want to do moments, when someone wants help completing a task or trying something new and lastly, I want to buy moments, when someone is ready to make a purchase and may need help deciding what to buy or how to buy it. Understanding these micro-moments within your own consumer journeys will help you to deliver on the consumers' needs and drive tangible action.

Microblogging

Microblogging is a combination of blogging and instant messaging that allows users to create short messages to be posted and shared with an audience online, typically done on the go! The social media platform Twitter could be described as a microblogging platform, along with Tumblr and Instagram, albeit their focus is more on visual content. The core benefits of microblogging include the quick time taken to create content, often on the fly, more frequent posts, a great way to share time sensitive and urgent information and of course mobile convenience. Consumers today are digesting content much more frequently than ever before, but in much shorter sharper, more bite sized chunks, so ensuring microblogging is part of your digital strategy is key!

Microsite

Essentially a microsite is a small website, micro if you will! Typically, companies and brands setup microsites to support specific campaigns, events, product launches etc. A microsite will have its own URL and is often not a permanent fixture, normally removed from the internet once the promotion is over or the information is no longer relevant.

Millennials

Ok so this term isn't just used in relation to digital, but it certainly is used a lot! Millennials are the generation of people born between the 1980s-2000s, digital natives! There is massive debate on their work ethics and how to communicate with them...I'll leave you to find out the rest!

Mobile Application

A mobile application, or app as we like to call them, is a type of application designed to run specifically on a mobile device, such as a smart phone or tablet. Mobile applications are normally categorized according to whether they are web-based or native apps, which are created specifically for a given platform. Mobile apps need to be created specifically for the operating system in which they will run, the main two platforms being iOS for Apple and Google's Android. Typically apps are downloaded from mobile app stores such as Google Play and the Apple App Store, although many websites today provide direct download links.

Multisensory Marketing

Most marketing efforts have traditionally focused on the visual experience and engagement, neglecting the other senses. Multisensory marketing looks to correct that by creating enriching environments that excite the fuller spectrum of senses. Advanced innovative tech like VR can help to touch other senses and create a multisensory environment, although I am yet to see the power of scent used well!

N is for Native

Native Advertising

Native advertising best describes content that is published in a publication, typically online, that resembles the publications editorial content but is actually paid for by an advertiser and used to promote the advertiser's products or services.

Negative Keywords

Negative keywords should be selected as part of your SEM or PPC campaign when using AdWords. These keywords are best described as words or phrases that are irrelevant to your campaign that that you do not want your ads to be displayed against when a user searches using these terms. For example, if one of your negative keywords is the word 'free' you are essentially telling AdWords not to show your ad's whenever the word 'free' is included in the search query.

Netiquette

I swear I am not making this up!!! Netiquette is a word used to describe the etiquette of the internet, covering best practice such as, don't spam people!

Net Promoter Score (NPS)

Net promoter score is used to measure customer experience and predict business growth, it is a key metric that is used as part of a customer experience program and should be complimented with other metrics and insights from additional touch points along a consumer journey. Understanding your NPS will help to give you a comprehensive, actionable view of the performance of your customer experience.

News Feed

Those of you old enough will remember that the News Feed as we all know it today started life off as the 'wall'. The news feed that we know today is a list of updates on your social media homepage. The news feed typically shows updates about those people and brands who are in your friends list or who you are following on your platform. News feeds are no longer just limited to Facebook, we have a news feed on other social platforms such as Twitter, Instagram and LinkedIn.

News Jacking

News Jacking refers to the practice of aligning a particular brand with a current news worthy event or story in an attempt to generate awareness, attention and boost the overall exposure of the brand. This is a technique that is typically used on social media platforms to help generate buzz and talk ability.

Newsroom

Traditionally, a newsroom was the place where journalists, reporters, editors, staffers and others worked together to craft news stories. Today, social newsrooms work in a similar fashion except they are designed to work online instead of within a physical location. Now websites have media centers aimed at fulfilling this need.

A social newsroom is set up online to help people find information to craft their stories, every newsroom has its own personality and features, but generally offers a variety of information. You can visit newsrooms or create one of your own to help people find your information to use in their stories

O is for Operating System

Omnichannel

Omnichannle is essentially a multichannel approach to sales and marketing and provides the end customers with a seamless shopping experience, regardless of whether the customer is shopping online, from a laptop, mobile device, telephone or on the ground. For an experience to be truly omnichannel there needs to be tight integration between each channel and back end technology. On-demand services from companies like Netflix and Spotify offer a great omnichannel experience, albeit without then offline element!

Operating System (OS)

An operating system is the core program/platform that manages all other programs on a computer or mobile device. The most common desktop operating systems include Microsoft Windows, Mac OS and Linu. The most common mobile operating systems include iOS, Android and Windows 10.

Opt-In

Opt-In is a term used to describe a list of people/contacts on a database who have opted in to receiving information and content, typically including things such as newsletters, company updates etc

Opt-Out

Opt-Out refers to the process of ensuring consumers have the option to opt-out and leave a particular communication. Typically you should always give consumers the option to opt-out of any communication from your brand.

Organic Traffic

Organic traffic is the complete opposite to paid traffic, which is sumarised by website traffic that is paid for by paid ads. Essentially organic traffic is driven to a website via organic search or by coming to a website directly, thus not costing the advertiser any money to acquire.

Outbound Marketing

Outbound marketing is the opposite to inbound marketing and refers to any kind of marketing activity where a brand initiates the conversation with its target consumer by sending an outbound message, this is typically done using email or even direct messaging platforms such as WhatsApp.

P is for Pixel

pCommerce

pCommerce stands for Participatory commerce, a model that allows shoppers to participate in the design, selection or funding of the products that they purchase. Kickstarter is a great example of this where customers determine whether a product gets made by contributing to the funding goal.

Page Impressions

Page impressions are a key metric for measuring the success of your website or web pages. These impressions are measured by the exact number of times a specific web page or site has been accessed or viewed by a user. A page impression acts as a counter for web pages/sites, helps to inform you how many times your site has been visited, in some cases these impressions are also called hits!

Page Title

Page titles are used as part of an SEO strategy. Every single webpage on a website has its own title. Typically the page title is part of the HTML code of a webpage and appears in the title bar of the browser. Search engines also display page titles in their search results. When creating a site and as part of your

SEO strategy it is important that when you write your page titles that these are optimized with search volume and intent.

Page Views

Page views is essentially another word for impressions. Once a new user lands on your website they will typically click on multiple pages. Each individual page a user clicks on and views is classed as a page view. Page views are a common metric to track using your web analytics tool. As a benchmark you would typically look for a single user to view at least 2 plus pages per visit.

Paid Traffic

Paid traffic is best described as the process of sending visitors to your website using paid means, this includes social media ads, ppc ads or even display ads on display networks. The purpose of paid traffic is to acquire new customers and drive volume traffic to a particular web based destination. Paid traffic is typically used at the lower end of the sales funnel and a great way to capture people who are in buying cycle and to drive qualified traffic as part of your eCommerce strategy.

Pay Per Click (PPC)

Pay-Per-Click, PPC or SEM marketing as it is sometimes known is a model of website marketing whereby organisations pay on a per click basis with their advertisements. Essentially as an advertiser you only pay when someone clicks on your advert and visits your site. PPC advertising as part of a search strategy and leveraging ad space on a search engine like Google is one of the most popular forms of PPC. When setting up a PPC campaign advertisers are able to bid for their particular ad placement, typically the more you bid the higher up your ad will be placed.

Performance Marketing

Performance marketing is a method of paid digital marketing whereby advertisers and brans pay when a specific action has been completed, such as an online sale or a lead form completed. Typically performance marketing is used in line with an eCommcere strategy and needs to be monitored very carefully to ensure improved ROI over a campaign lifecycle.

Periscope

Periscope is an application that lets you share and experience live video content streams directly from your smartphone or tablet. The app is ideal for sharing live content such as sporting events, news stories or even music concerts. Unlike traditional video content Periscope encourages users to participate in real time with the video content, this is normally done through the sending of comments from viewers to the person sharing the content.

Permalink

A permalink is another word for a permanent link or a URL that always points and directs users to the same web page or site. Permalinks are also a key part of blogging and SEO strategy. In this instance they are used as backlinks to the primary domain as well as internal links to posts within a website.

PHP

Ready for a techie answer??? Ok so Php is an HTML embedded web scripting language. PHP code is normally inserted into the HTML of a web page. PHP code is then transformed into HTML before a page is loaded, users would never actually see PHP code when looking at a site. PHP is one of the most common development languages and has a number of unique features and functions. The main focus of PHP is to allow web developers to write dynamic pages quickly and easily, it is also great for enabling database driven content.

Pinterest

Pinterest is a social media platform that allows users the opportunity to create, curate and share images that have been found online, essentially acting as a visual bookmarking tool. Pinterest launched in 2010 and like Facebook was invitation only to begin with, the site now boasts well over 200 million users on a monthly basis.

Pixel

A pixel in digital marketing terms has a couple of meanings. In its original form a pixel is the smallest unit of a digital image or graphic that can be displayed on a digital device, also known as a picture element. The other meaning for the word pixel relates to paid media and tracking. Pixel based tracking is the process of using a 1x1 pixel to track a visit or event on a webpage to track impressions, web visits, conversions etc. Utilizing this form of ad tracking is ideal for supporting cookie based tracking and retargeting.

Plug-In

A plug-in best describes an application that can easily be implemented and used as part of your web browser. The most popular plug-in has to be Adobe's Acrobat, the document presentation and navigation program that lets you view documents just as they look as a print ready file. Plug-in applications are recognized automatically by the web browser and its function is integrated into the main HTML file that is being presented.

PockeTVC

A PockeTVC is Facebooks answer to today's online, mobile television commercial. This ad type takes existing TV assets and fits them for mobile. Due to terrestrial television viewership's dropping and the increase in video consumption on social channels the PockeTVC is a great way to ensure your television commercial assets can reach an audience on the go via social.

Podcast

The word Podcast actually originates from the combination of two other words, iPod and broadcast. A podcast is an audio or video broadcast that is typically played on an iPod or iPhone and are downloaded using Apple iTunes. Podcasts are distributed by both businesses and personal amateur producers who want to share their content with others. Many news organisations also offer podcasts of their news stories and programs. Podcasts are typically distributed in 'episodes' meaning that new podcasts are often made available on regular basis.

Pop-Up Ad

A pop-up ad is an ad that usually pops up in a separate window, typically these ads are initiated when a user completes a particular action such as opening a webpage, clicking on a link or hovering a mouse over a certain part of a web page. Like all pop-ups a pop-up ad is always smaller than the background interface and often resembles a small browser window with only the close, minimize and maximize options at the top. Pop-up ads are not popular with the typical internet user as they often cause disruption to the users online experience, there are several products available that can be used to disable this form of advertising.

Portal

A web portal is a specifically designed website or web page that often serves as the single point of access for information on a particular subject. Web portals are accessible from multiple platforms such as desktop PCs, smartphones and other mobile devices. Some of the main features of a web portal include data access, personal content, transactional information and published content. Web based portals can also present content and information based on a particular users profile and can typically handle both structured and unstructured content. Web portals can also be used to display specific information such as analytics reports and business intelligence data.

Print Media

Oops – wrong book! Print media, or traditional advertising is a dying art, newspapers, magazines, posters and direct mail are all considered as print media. Whilst there may be a role for print media today it is limited. Across the globe organizations are shifting large sums of their marketing budget to digital, as the phrase goes 'you need to fish where the fish are'.

Privacy Policy

No doubt you have seen these on websites from time to time. A privacy policy is a statement or legal document that discloses some or all of the ways an organization collects, uses, discloses and manages consumer data and information. Almost all websites make their privacy policy available to site visitors so that there is complete transparency on how consumer data will be and can be used.

Probablistic

Probablistic is a term used to describe the use of data points to guess who the consumer is on the other side of the screen. Knowing where a person is, what time it is and the device in use help, but not with nearly 100% confidence. This type of data is usually considered less accurate that deterministic, though many say a blend of the two provide the most accurate results.

Programmatic

Programmatic advertising helps to automate the decision making process of media buying by targeting specific audiences and demographics. Programmatic ads are placed using artificial intelligence and real-time bidding for online display, social media advertising, mobile and video campaigns and is even expanding to traditional tv advertising.

Q is for Qwerty

Quality Score

Quality Score is the metric that Google uses to determine your page ranking and how much you should pay per click in a particular AdWords marketing campaign. The quality scores is essentially a measurement of relevance; more relevant ads, campaigns and landing pages have much higher click through rates, which in turn raises your quality score. No one who works outside of Google knows exactly how the quality socre algorithm works, but we do know that click-through rate is the most important component. When more people who see your ad click on it, that's a strong indication to Google that your ad is relevant and helpful to users. Generally speaking the higher your quality score, the lower your cost per conversion. The key thing to remember is that a high quality score is Googles way of saying that your PPC ad meets your potential consumer's needs. The better you are at reaching your consumer's needs, being relevant, the less Google will charge you for the ad click!

R is for Reach

Ranking

The word ranking, when used in context to SEO, refers to a websites position on a search engines results page. There are a number of different factors that help to influence a websites rank on a search engines, these typically come down to relevance of content based on the search term that a user has typed into a search bar, another key factor is the quality of backlinks that are pointing to the particular page. Ranking factors play an instrumental role in SEO and an organizations overall digital marketing strategy. The key for any brand should be to ensure that they rank on the first page of Google, ideally the top half for both brand related and broader relevant keyword searches. The utopia for any organization is to try and ensure that all the listings on the first page of Google point to your own assets, website, social media pages, pr articles and user reviews for example.

Reach

In digital marketing the term reach typically refers to how many different people have seen an online ad and the percentage of these people that fall into the audience to which the ad was targeting. You will often here media companies talking about estimated reach when looking to setup paid media campaigns on social channels, as well as

GDN and banner based advertising. If you are running a campaign that is focused on top of funnel brand awareness and you want to ensure your message is seen by as many people as possible you will want to ensure you have wide reach.

Real-time Engagement

Thanks to the high adoption levels of smart phones the modern day consumer is pretty much always online, one of the ways brands can cut through existing content and create noise and impact is through real-time engagement. Social platforms like Facebook and Instagram are great platforms for brands to engage with their consumers in real-time, Instagram Stories and Facebook Live are primes examples of how brands can leverage these platforms to speak to and engage in conversation with fans, followers and prospects. Real live story telling is quite a skill and requires brands to prep in advance as well as be able to adapt their content on the fly in real-time.

Reddit

Reddit is a popular social media news website and forum where content is socially curated and promoted through online voting, I believe that the site's name is actually a play on the words 'I read it'. Reddit site members, also known as redditors, submit content which is then voted upon by other reddit members, the main goal is to send well-regarded content to the top of the sites front page. The more votes that a piece of content gets the higher up it appears!

Retargeting

Retargeting, or remarketing as it is also know, is a form of digital advertising that can help you keep your brand in fro not bounced traffic after they have left your website. For most websites only a very small percentage of traffic actually converts on its first visit. Retargeting is a tool that allows companies reach users who don't convert straight away and drive them back to your site. Retargeting is a very powerful branding and conversion rate optimization tool but it works best if it is part of a much larger digital strategy. Retargeting works best when used in conjunction with other inbound and outbound marketing strategies. The likes of PPC, AdWords, display banners are great at generating awareness and even driving traffic through to a website. However, they often fail to drive quality conversions. Retargeting can be used to help increase conversion, but it can't drive cold users to your site! Retargeting can be of particular use as part of an eCommerce strategy, a great way to re-engage with users who have added items to a basket but not completed their purchase would be through retargeting.

Retweet

If you aren't a big Twitter user, then chances are the word retweet maybe a little foreign to you. A retweet is when you republish a post that another Twitter user has written, to spread the word among your own Twitter followers. Its essentially a way of amplifying content so that more and more people can see the original message. Retweeting is not only great for your followers and for spreading news, it is also a great way to build a relationship with the original poster, who can easily see who has retweeted him or her. People who post and repost effectively can build a following of millions!

Rich Media

Rich media is an online advertising term for web based ads that use advanced technology such as streaming video and content that instantly interacts with a user, often these ads are set to play when a user opens a particular webpage or when they hover their mouse over them. Standard graphic base ads using formats such as JPEG and GIF would not be classed as rich media. Video content, Flash content and Shockwave content would be classed as rich media.

RSS Feed

RSS is a format for delivering regularly changing web content. Many news-related sites, blogs and other online publishers syndicate their content as an RSS Feed to whoever wants it. An RSS Reader is then required to collect the feeds and display them for you to use.

RSS Reader

To follow on from above an RSS Reader OR News Aggregator software allows you to grab an RSS feed from various sites and display the information for you to read. There is a variety of RSS readers that are available for different platforms. Once you have your Feed Reader, it's just a matter finding sites that syndicate content and adding their RSS feed to the list of feeds your feed reader checks.

S is for Selfie

Search Engine

In its simplest form a search engine is a web site that collects and organizes content from all over the internet. As a user if we want to locate something or find out specific information a search engine is one of the first places we would go. Google is by far the number on search engine used today, albeit there are a handful of other options available such as Bing and Yahoo. Today the content categorization on the search engines is all about relevance. These platforms are designed to ensure that as consumers we are able to locate information and content in as fewer steps as possible. The Google search engine has a number of great additional features such as reviews, images, buy-now, maps, phone numbers, news articles, the list goes on and on!

Search Engine Optimization (SEO)

Search Engine Optimisation, or SEO as it is more commonly known is a methodology of strategies, techniques, people and tactics that are used to increase the number of website visitors by obtaining a high ranking on a search engine. There are so many factors that help to determine a website position and ranking in a search engines results, including content, keyword relevance, social metrics, domain name, sitemaps, search console and backlinks – I could literally write a book on this subject alone!

Search Query

A search query in internet terms is the query that a user enters into a search engine when looking for information on the internet. The words that are used act as keywords that the search engine uses to algorithmically match relevant results to. These results are displayed on the search engine results pages in order of relevance.

Second Screen

The second screen refers to smartphones or tablets that are used whilst watching traditional television. In some cases these second screens can be used to connect with the program tat the user is watching on the television, typically through a native app, the smartphone or tablet then becomes a television companion device. Whilst the traditional television broadcasting industry continues to struggle this use of innovation could help to create an exciting digital engagement opportunity for users, mixing traditional and digital devices!

Selfie

The modern-day self-portrait. Not necessarily a digital marketing term but with the development of social media and the smartphone I couldn't miss this one out! A selfie for anyone living under a rock for the past few years is essentially a picture taken yourself that is planned to be uploaded to social media. You can usually see the persons arm in the photograph unless they are a professional selfie taker and have in fact invested in a selfie stick!

Sequential Messaging

Sequential messaging describes the process of hitting a consumer with one message, then a different one, and then another to guide them toward making a purchase or taking a desired action. Sequential messaging, also known as sequential targeting, often required cross device capabilities to accurately reach the same consumer across different screens when they visit different digital assets.

SERP

There are literally billions of websites and web pages that exist on the internet today but from a digital marketing perspective some of the most important are those that are on the search engine results pages, or SERPs as they are also known! Search engine results pages are the web pages that are presented to users after they have searched for something on a search engine like Google. Every single SERP is completely unique, even if a search query is performed on the same search engine using the same keywords. This is because all search engines customize the user experience for their users by presenting results based on many factors, this includes things like the consumers search history, their location and their social settings. Whilst brands can buy their way to page one of search results using paid advertising spots the goal is to organically earn the right to have your web assets on page one of Google for relevant search queries.

Server

In its simplest form a server is a computer, a device or a program that is dedicated to managing a network or internet resource. You will often notice that servers are dedicated to a particular task, for example you will have a print server, email server, web server, file server and database server. Typically dedicated servers have high performance RAM, a fast processer and often need to be very reliable due to their business related functions. In some organisations these servers are housed in 'server rooms' often air cooled and content on these servers is typically backed up on a regular basis to ensure no loss of information or downtime.

Sessions

User sessions refers to the number of unique users who have visited a particular website over a specified period of time. Measuring user sessions is an important metric when looking at site traffic KPIs and measuring the success of your various online media activities.

Siri

Siri, like Alexa and Google Assistant, is a voice recognition service, this time applied to Apple devices and iOS operating systems. Siri like other voice recognition services responds to spoken questions by speaking back to the user and presenting the relevant information from certain applications. Siri can also be used to help dictate emails, text messages and can even read emails and messages back to the user.

Site Map

A site map is a visual, or text based representation of the organized content on a web site. This allows users to navigate through the site to find information that they are looking for, just as a traditional road map can help people find a locations. A site map is a useful tool to help designers when building a site, it is also a great way to demonstrate how a site works, consumer journey mapping across a site and even to help content writers know where to put particular elements of a site. When a site is live search engines use the site map to help crawl the site for pages and content to ensure that individual pages are indexed, and consumers can find relevant information with ease.

Skins

In digital marketing terms a skin is a graphic or audio file that is used to change the appearance of a user interface, like a website. From an advertising perspective a background skin is an ad format whereby the advert frames an existing webpage. This is also known as background advertising, page skins or wallpaper advertising. This form of advertising is often used for particular promotions such as product launches or to support particular events or sponsorship.

Skype

Skype is an online telephony service provider that offers free calling between users across the internet. Skype also enable video chat, file transfers, instant messaging and even video conferencing. The skype application is available on desktop computers, laptops, tablets and even smartphones. At one stage you could even purchase dedicated skype telephones.

Skyscraper

A skyscraper advert is a tall and narrow online banner advertisement that is usually placed on the right hand side of a web page. Along with banner ads and MPUs skyscrapers are one of the most common sized online banner ads available today.

SlideShare

SlideShare is the sister company to the social media platform LinkedIn. It is the most popular platform for sharing presentations and other knowledge based content online. SlideShare is a great marketing tool for companies who want to share valuable content with consumers and other individuals. From a consumer perspective SlideShare is a great place to go when looking for insights and information on a specific business-related topic.

Smart Content

Smart content can also be referred to as dynamic content, typically this content will sit on a website and will change based on the interests or past behavior of a user. The purpose of smart content is to help provide a more relevant and personalized customer experience to users than that of static content. A great example of this is with the Amazon website, using past purchase history Amazon is able to make recommendations and predictions, thus providing consumers with a personalized and relevant shopping experience.

Snackable Content

Due to the rise and popularity of mobile devices we as consumers have a diminishing attention span. We no longer have the time to sit down and read reels and reels of content and data, instead we digest data and content on the go, in snackable, bite sized chunks! Snackable content!

Snapchat

Snapchat is a social media platform/mobile application that allows users to send and receive 'self-destructing' photo and video content, these photos and videos are called snaps! There are a number of different functions available on Snapchat including Snapchat stories, Snapchat memories and Snapchat filters. Snapchat was also one of the first social platforms to leverage augmented reality through their dancing hotdog character!

Social Amplification

Social amplification is best described by the process of getting a message amplified through staff, customers, partners, fans, followers and influencers. Each individual sharer extends your message and ultimately your reach to their own personal network of fans and followers, who can then in turn promote and amplify the message on and so on. Ensuring you are working with the right influencers and customers can help to ensure that you gain maximum reach and potential virality. This form of advertising is great for raising awareness and helps to create real social buzz and chatter.

Social Analytics

Social analytics is the process of gathering data and information from social media sites and analyzing the data using social media analytics tools to support wider marketing activity. Setting KPIs is a key element to measuring success on social media and analytics reports enable brands to track and trace every element of their social strategies to ensure they are in line with their KPIs and constantly refining activity to improve performance.

Social Bookmarking

Social bookmarking is the process of tagging a web page with a web-based tool so that you can easily access it later. Instead of saving to your web browser, you are saving them to the internet, and, because your bookmarks are online you can easily access them anywhere you have an internet connection. The most popular social bookmarking tools include Delicious, Pinterest, Bitly and Evernote.

Social Commerce

Social commerce is a subset of traditional ecommerce that involves social media and other online media that supports social interaction, ultimately assisting in online buying and selling. As social continues to drive the majority of online activity you can break social commerce down even further into the following elements, peer-to-peer sales platforms, eBay, Etsy and online marketplaces, Social network-driven sales, Facebook, Twttier etc, Group Buying, like Groupon, user curated shopping and pCommerce.

Social CRM

Social CRM describes the process of consumer engagement through social sites such as Twitter and Facebook. Typically social CRM integrates social media platforms with customer relationship management systems to provide insight into customer interactions with a brand, and to improve the quality of customer engagement. Social CRM can be used to form a personalized marketing strategy that is seen as non-intrusive and more engagement based. Social CRM helps to create new customers, provide quicker customer service and enable customers to share their experience with millions online.

Social Listening

Social media listening, or social media monitoring as it is also known is the process of identify and assessing what is being spoken about by individuals on social media platforms. Conversations on social media, social chatter, produces a huge amount of data and information that is very important to brands. However, identifying and listening to this chatter requires the use of social listening tools. Monitoring consumer behavior and conversation on social media platforms is a great way to understand what your consumers are talking about, what brands they are discussing, the sentiment of these conversations and where the discussions are taking place.

Social Media

Social media is the name given to websites and applications that allow users the ability to create, curate and share content and to participate in social networking. The main players in social media include Facebook, Twitter, Google+, Wikipedia, LinkedIn, Instagram, Snapchat, Reddit and Pinterest. Social media sites have moved from being purely entertainment based to an integral part of our lives, almost a utility. Brands have jumped on the social bandwagon as a cost effective way to raise awareness, acquire customers and build one to one communication with their advocates. Social media should be a key element to any digital marketing strategy.

Social Selling

Social selling is when brands and sales people leverage social media platforms to interact directly with their prospects. The practice of social selling is typically used within a B2B environment and platforms like LinkedIn offer a number of social selling tools to aid the process. Social selling ensures that sales people are able to engage with prospects in a slightly softer manner than traditional methods such as cold calling and direct mail, helping to build solid relationships and over time loyal customers.

SoLoMo

Social, local and mobile! SoLoMo is the convergence of social collaboration, location-based targeting and on the go mobile technology! SoLoMo applications allow advertisers to push notifications to potential customers who are geographically nearby. The SoLoMo principles are also increasingly being used and incorporated into search engines to ensure queries deliver location based results to users.

Spam

The word spam refers to email that is typically classed as junk, junk mail if you will. You could even go as far as to say that any email that is unsolicited is called as spam. Typically, the term spam is referred to when used to describe advertising or sales based emails, especially those that are not relevant. The reason spam mail is such an issue is that it essentially wastes peoples time with unwanted content, it can also eat into network bandwidth. Many email programs such as Outlook and Gmail offer spam filters to help ensure inbox's are clogged up with unwanted mail.

Spotify

Spotify is a digital music service that enables users to remotely source millions of different songs from their laptop, tablet or smartphone. One of the main features of Spotify is the ability to setup and share music and playlists with others. This is great for setting up specific playlists that tie back to your brand or wider marketing activity. Spotify users can send and share music via social media platforms or through email!

SSP

An SSP, or supply-side platform as it is also known, is a software system that allows publishers to offer their available inventory to ad exchanges and DSPs. Supply side refers to the supply of advertising space, which is what the publisher is offering advertisers. Traditionally the publisher has been a website owner but today could also be an app developer. SSPs and DSPs are the two core entities involved in programmatic buying, automating the processes around purchase and placement of ads through real-time bidding (RTB).

Staging Link/Site

A staging link or staging site as it is also known is essentially a staging site that lets you do user testing on your website, and make modifications to content and functionality before pushing your website live to end consumers. Typically staging sites sit on a staging URL to ensure that people do not access the site. When doing user testing it is important to ensure that tests are carried out on multiple browsers and devices.

Storytelling

Digital storytelling is merely the modern day version of traditional storytelling. Typically, today digital storytelling refers to the practice of everyday people using digital technology to tell their stories, blogs are a great example of this! Digital stories are typically not professional productions, and because of this are not seen as advertisements, making them far more emotive, intimate and authentic. Using influencers to help amplify your message through digital stories is a great way to reach communities.

Streaming

Streaming is a common practice on the internet today and typically involves audio or video based content being played back without being completely downloaded first. With streaming media a user does not need to fully download the file to play it. The media is sent to the user in a continuous stream of data and can be played as it arrives. Streaming media technology has improved massively. However, the quality of the streamed content is still hugely dependent on the end users connection speed.

T is for Twitter

Tag management

Tag management is the process of managing online marketing activity through tracking tags, typically done using something like Google Tag Manager. Tags are snippets of code that are usually placed on a page to enable 3rd party tracking, analysis and reporting. Google Analytics and other analytics platforms are able to provide tags, others include remarketing, conversion tracking and affiliates.

Time on site

When using web based analytics tools, such as Google Analytics, one of the key metrics that you should be looking to track is 'time on site'. This metric measures the average amount of time a user spends on your site, typically in minutes and seconds. Depending on the type of site that you have a good benchmark for time on site should be around 4 minutes. If your time on site is lower than this it is important to understand why. Why are people leaving, is it lack of content, page load time or lack of consumer journey?

Traffic

The term traffic, with regards to digital marketing, refers to the web site traffic, the number of visits and visitors that a web site receives. Web site traffic is quite a basic measure, whilst it is important to ensure that your web assets have high traffic the quality of this traffic is of more importance, especially when looking at conversions.

Trending Topic

A trending topic is a particular subject matter that is experiencing a surge in popularity on one or more social media platforms. Typically these trending topics are measured by high use of a particular hashtag. Understanding these trending topics can help you to understand consumer behavior and drive content creation to ensure you are creating 'on trend' content that is likely to be relevant at this moment in time.

Trendjacking

Trendjacking describes the process of capitalizing on a particular trend in order to provide additional exposure for your brand, in some cases the trend is manipulated or changed to bring to light a new story, message, idea or product. Memes are a great way to jump on a particular trend, they can be created very quickly and are often seen as highly shareable, especially if covering a popular, relevant, trending topic.

Tumblr

Tumblr is a free social networking website that allows users to post multimedia content to their own customizable blogs. Tumblr is best suited for broadcasting short messages and bite sized content to readers, a microblogging platform. Each Tumblr blog is referred to as a tumbleblog and users can post text, images, videos, links and audio files. The platform has over 70 million blogs, 30 billion posts and 16 billion monthly page views, mostly by people aged 35 and under!

Tweet

In its simplest form a Tweet is a post on Twitter. I believe the name tweet originates from the fact that a tweet is limited to only 280 characters, and the word tweet resembles the same type of short and sweet chirp you might here from a bird! Like Facebook you can also share media rich links on Twitter such as images and videos.

Twitter

Twitter is one of the largest and most popular social networking and microblogging sites used today. Twitter members are able to broadcast short posts, tweets, and follow other users. Twitter is increasingly being used by organisations, albeit its purpose is sometimes better aligned to channels such as news, pr and customer service, as opposed to outbound marketing activity. Functionality includes paid media, boosted posts and content, image and video content and of course Twitter is home to the hashtag!

U is for URL

Unique Users

In digital marketing terms a unique users is a distinct individual who has viewed a website or web page. Unique users are measured by the IP address associated with their computer or mobile device. Marketers track unique users to determine how many actual people see their content within a given period of time. The number of unique users that are served specified content is typically referred to as that contents reach!

URL

URLs are a set of characters used to identify a particular resource, like a website, over the internet. Common URL protocols include HTTP and HTTPS for websites, MAILTO for email and FTP for file transfer. Typically URLs are used to pint to a particular website or webpage and often contain a particular domain name.

User Centered Design (UCD)

User centered design is a design process that focusses on the end users' needs and requirements. Typically, this approach should be used when building digital assets such as a website or mobile application. The core aim of user centered design is to ensure high user satisfaction with the end product. In order to ensure you follow a UCD design approach it is imperative that you have explicit understanding of your consumers, their needs, requirements, habits, pain points, tasks and fully understand their environment.

User Experience (UX)

In summary user experience best describes every single aspect of an end user/consumers interaction with your brand, product or services. In digital marketing terms understanding a user's experience with your brand is of key importance, this includes their experience across all touchpoints, social media, online advertising, websites and applications. When looking at your digital assets it is important to look at the overall end user experience, a good way to test this is with actual customers. Understanding how they feel, usability, functionality, and overall pleasure that they experience when interacting with your brand will help you to tweak design and process elements to ensure optimal user engagement.

User Generated Content (UGC)

User generated content is best defined as any type of online content that has been created by unpaid contributors, or end consumers. UGC can refer to pictures, videos, testimonials, product reviews, memes, tweets, blog posts and pretty much every other content type you can think of! As consumers, we are becoming more and more savvy when it comes to brands and paid content, user generated content is often seen as far more authentic, real and transparent. Typically, users who generate content have a strong feeling towards a brand, they are doing so without payment and are therefore often seen as fans or advocates, rewarding and recognizing these users should be a key focal point of your content strategy.

User Interface (UI)

Often referred to as UI a user interface is one of the most important parts of any web based program, such as a website. One of the main types of user interface is called a graphical user interface. This includes touch screen interfaces, mobile application interfaces, website interfaces or even the interface on a computer game or social platform.

V is for Viral

View Through Rate (VTR)

View through rate of an online advert is a common metric used for measuring the success of content and a campaign. In summary VTR is the percentage of people who saw an ad all the way through, out of those who had the advert load on their computer. View through rate typically applies to video-based content, it is a great measure to keep an eye on with your YouTube based content. Video is one of the most consumed content types online today so should form a key element of your content strategy. However, consumer time is tight, ensuring that consumers are watching all of your video content is key, if they are not watching video content all the way through you may want to look at shorter more succinct content.

Views

In digital marketing terms views can relate to a number of topics such as page views, video views, social content and live content views. Regardless of the application views is a basic measurement that can sometimes be taken out of context. Whilst it may seem important to get a high number of views these need to be quality views that translate into actionable business or conversions. Ensuring you have the right call to action with your content will ensure that these views convert into something much more solid.

Vimeo

Vimeo, a lot like YouTube, is a video sharing website that allows users to view, upload and share video based content. Vimeo offers users a number of creative tools to help enhance video content, this includes add music tracks. In addition to this Vimeo also has a number of business-based options such as Vimeo Plus, Vimeo Pro and Vimeo for business, these help to give better search engine visibility and also the option to remove third party advertising.

Viral

The term viral refers to a piece of digital content such as a video, image or article that has spiked in popularity and has reached a large number of users in a very short space of time. Whilst there is no 'exact number' of views that makes something go viral most viral media is viewed by more than one million people in less than a week. The most common type of viral media is videos, typically hosted on a platform like YouTube. For a video to become viral it needs to reach a certain threshold, once it reaches this level of popularity the number of views spike upwards and the video becomes viral. Whilst video content can be pushed through paid media, viral content typically explodes due to consumers sharing the content themselves, thus making it viral.

Virtual Reality

Virtual reality is an artificially created environment that has been created using computer software and technology and is presented to an end user in such a way that the user believes it to be a real environment. In its simplest form virtual reality is a 3D image that can be explored interactively on a desktop computer. In more recent years there has been an explosion of wrap around based VR applications that are viewed on mobile devices. This wearable technology is the future and can be applied to any brand to help improve customer experience and create distinct consumer engagement. A great application of this technology could be in the real-estate sector, using VR to provide prospects with a real life view of property that has not yet been built or is in another country is a great way to engage and sell!

Virus

A computer virus is a malicious software program loaded on to a user's computer, without the user knowing, and performs malicious actions. One thing to note is that computer virus, unlike human virus', never occur naturally., they are always induced by people. Most computer viruses perform actions that are malicious in nature, such as destroying data and are typically transferred from one user to another through a network or email communication. Ensuring you have up-to-date anti-virus software stored on machines is of paramount importance.

Visualisation

The term visualization actually refers to video content. Video content is the number one consumed content on the internet today and brands are increasingly looking at ways in which they can implement video-based content into their marketing strategies. Video content is far more engaging than traditional text and images and therefore also highly shareable.

Vlog

A vlog is simply a blog that contains video content. This is the largest growing segment of the blogosphere and is driven by our thirst for video content. Some bloggers have included video content for years. However, vlogging has become more and more common as equipment prices have dropped and sites like YouTube provide a great platform for promoting vlogs. Mainstream media like terrestrial television is on the decline in many parts around the world, as a result we spend more and more time on the internet watching on demand video based content, tapping into vloggers should be a key element to your influencer strategy.

W is for WWW

Wearable Tech

We've all heard of Google glasses, Fitbits and the Galaxy Gear. All of these are described as wearable tech, technology that you wear!

Webcasting

Webcasting is a term that refers to broadcasting or presenting of content over the internet. Platforms like social media have helped to drive webcasting, particularly that in real time. Webcasting can cover everything from PowerPoint presentations presented over a webinar through to real-time sports results and news broadcasting utilizing tools like Facebook Live and Instagram Stories.

Webinar

A webinar is best described as an educational, informative or instructional presentation that is made available online, usually as either video, audio or PowerPoint. Webinar attendees connect online, typically using internet based webinar technology to help enhance the overall experience through instant messaging, file sharing and social engagement. The word webinar actually comes from two other words….web and seminar ☺

Website

A website is a collection of online files that include a lead or beginning file that is typically called a homepage. There is well over 1 billion websites on the internet today and they are all accessed by a user's web browser. As consumers spend more and more time online a website is a key element to any digital marketing strategy, no matter how small or large your business. Ensuring you have a key strategy and objective for your website is key, do you want to use your site as an online information resource, an online shop, a booking agent, an online gallery, the opportunities are endless.

WeChat

WeChat is a social media and instant messaging platform service that has been developed in China, it is one of the largest standalone messaging applications by monthly active users. WeChat has a number of features including text messaging, hold-to-talk, voice messaging, broadcast messaging, video conferencing, video games, image and video sharing and location sharing. There is also a business based application of WeChat called Enterprise WeChat. If as a brand you are looking to engage with a Chinese market this is the number one social platform to help you reach potential customers!

White Hat

The term white hat refers to SEO and the usage of strategies, techniques and processes that focus specifically on a human audience. White hat SEO is also sometimes referred to as ethical SEO, examples of its application include using keywords, keyword analysis, back-linking, link building and writing content for consumers.

Wireframe

Wireframes are an important tool used in the process of website development. Wireframes are used as a visualization tool for presenting proposed layout, functionality, structure and content of a website or webpage. A wireframe is also used to separate the graphical elements of a website from the functional elements to help web teams easily explain how users will interact.

Word OF Mouth (WOM)

Word of mouth marketing has been around for quite some time, and the digital world has made it even bigger than before. What used to be friends sharing tips on the best deals around town while grabbing a coffee is now a world wide web of friends liking, sharing, and commenting on their next favorite thing.

X is for Xylophone

XML

XML stands for Extensible Markup Language (geek alert) and is used to describe data. The XML standard is a flexible and convenient way to create information formats and electronically share structured data via the internet.

Y is for YouTube

YouTube

YouTube is the number one free video hosting website that allows users the ability to upload, store and share video content. YouTube users and visitors can share YouTube videos on a variety of different platforms by using a link or by embedding HTML code. Traditionally most of the videos on YouTube have been created by amateurs. However, the platform is increasingly being used by professional film makers and brands who are looking to share their work. Virtually every genre of video exists on YouTube, music, video, how-to guides, you name it, its on there! YouTube is also the second largest search engine used today, it is important to remember that when uploading video content to YouTube that you must optimize the title and description for search, ensuring that your video reaches its audience and has good viewership.

Z is for Zuckerberg

Zombie Cookie

A zombie cookie is a normal browser cookie that returns back after being deleted by the user or by dedicated software. A zombie cookie will traditionally be recreated by a flash cookie when it is deleted.

So there you go, that's my A-Z of digital marketing terms, buzzwords and jargon. I am almost 100% sure that there are terms that I have missed, but as previously stated, that's how it works with digital, ever evolving and at lightning speed.

I hope this goes some way towards helping you in your marketing profession, I am sure I am not the only one wo has found themselves nodding along in a meeting, too afraid to ask, 'what do you mean?'.

It goes without saying that some of the explanations in this book are of course my own and therefore may be a little subjective! However, I've been doing this for a long time now and am pretty confident with the information provided here!

I'm going to leave you with a quote:

'Marketing is no longer about the stuff that you make, but about the stories that you tell'

With that in mind I hope some of the buzzwords in this book help you to write a great story of you own! Be successful. Be digital. Be a unicorn!